Audacity

A Play

Simon Mawdsley

A SAMUEL FRENCH ACTING EDITION

SAMUEL
FRENCH
FOUNDED 1830

SAMUELFRENCH-LONDON.CO.UK
SAMUELFRENCH.COM

ISBN 978-0-573-11039-9

www.samuelfrench-london.co.uk

www.samuelfrench.com

FOR AMATEUR PRODUCTION ENQUIRIES

UNITED KINGDOM AND WORLD EXCLUDING NORTH AMERICA

plays@SamuelFrench-London.co.uk

020 7255 4302/01

Each title is subject to availability from Samuel French,

depending upon country of performance.

AUDACITY

First performed at Barons Court Theatre, London in
October 1999 with the following cast:

Philip	Neil Bird
John	Steve Foster
Dave	Lee Barnes
Gillian	Kate Carthy
Gemma	Sharon Dungey

Directed by Simon Mawdsley
Designed by Brett Stevens

A revised version was performed at the Jermyn Street
Theatre in September 2004 with the following cast:

Philip	Neil Bird
John	James Petherick
Dave	Ian Attfield
Gillian	Hilary Burns
Gemma	Caroline George

Directed by Simon Mawdsley
Designed by Brett Stevens

CHARACTERS

Philip, late 30s
John, late 40s
Dave, mid-30s
Gillian, John's wife, early 40s
Gemma, Dave's wife, late 20s

SYNOPSIS OF SCENES

The action of the play takes place in a basement bedsit flat, somewhere in West London

Time — the present

ACT I

SCENE 1 A Friday evening in November
SCENE 2 A month later
SCENE 3 A week later. Eleven a.m.

ACT II

SCENE 1 Two minutes later
SCENE 2 A few mnutes later

This play is dedicated to
Bethany and Summer

AUTHOR'S NOTE

Although the play is set in London, it could, with a few adjustments, take place in any major city.

Grateful acknowledgements to: Jonathan Chinsky, Andrew Pegram, Mandy Wright, Mike Penketh, David Mawdsley, Paul Johnson and Caroline Petherbridge.

Simon Mawdsley

COPYRIGHT MUSIC

ACT 1
SCENE 1

A basement bedsit flat, somewhere in West London. A Friday evening in November

The flat is dingy and sparsely furnished. The front door opens to the steps from the street. Next to the door is a window with venetian blinds. A door, or doorway, leads through to the offstage kitchen and bathroom. A single, naked lightbulb hangs from the ceiling. There is a single fold-up bed with a bare mattress against the back wall and a kitchen table C with three chairs, none of which match. There is a chest of drawers or cabinet (with a bottle of Scotch and a stack of plastic cups on it) in one corner and an old radiator in another

There are spaces to either side of the bedsit set which will be used to suggest other rooms in Act I Scene 2

When the play begins, the light bulb is lit and a street lamp shines through the window

Philip enters from the kitchen. He is in his late thirties, dressed in trousers, a white shirt and a loosened tie. He is anxious. He checks his watch, goes to the window, turns up the radiator, checks his watch again. He goes over to the cabinet and pours himself a drink. He opens the top drawer of the cabinet, takes out a handgun and studies it for a moment, then puts it away and knocks back his Scotch in one gulp

There is a knock at the door. Philip takes a second to compose himself, then moves to the door

Philip (*opening the door*) John. Come in.

John enters. He is about ten years older than Philip, grey-haired, dressed in a sensible coat over a conservative suit and tie. He is well-mannered and a little nervous

John Thanks. Thank you. Sorry I'm late, Philip.
Philip You're not. As punctual as ever, in fact — bang on eight o'clock.
John Five past, by my watch.
Philip Find it OK?
John Yes. I walked straight past it, initially. Hadn't realized it was a basement flat.
Philip I did say.

John Did you? Sorry.

Philip Take your coat?

John D'you mind if I keep it on a while? Warm up a bit. Rather chilly out there.

Philip Not much warmer in here I'm afraid.

John Winter on its way.

Philip Drop of Scotch should do the trick.

John Scotch? Er, no thanks.

Philip You're not driving are you? Oh, no, of course you're not. Sorry.

John No, I came on the Underground. Can I be boring and just have a cup of tea? If that's at all possible?

Philip I'll put the kettle on. Scotch later, perhaps?

Philip exits into the kitchen

(*Off*) So, John, what do you reckon?

John Sorry?

Philip (*off*) The flat — what d'you think?

John Yes. It's very … erm …

Philip (*off*) It's a dump.

Philip appears in the doorway

Not fit for a cockroach.

John No. But — quite near to the tube station — which is quite handy, I expect. Are you renting or buying?

Philip Renting. Short term.

John Ah. Hence the lack of furnishings. So, erm, why … ?

Philip Why I should want to rent a place like this?

John I'm sure you have a good reason.

Philip Tea, was it?

John Tea, yes. Please. Thanks. Marvellous.

Philip exits again into the kitchen

Philip (*off*) How's Gilly?

John Gilly? Yes, she's fine. Fine. Despite all the … Got herself an evening job, to help out with the finances. Stacking shelves at Tesco's, would you believe? I mean, Gilly, of all people, stacking shelves, for goodness' sake. Just two nights a week — Mondays and Thursdays — says she enjoys it but, well … I don't know.

Philip (*off*) Every little helps.

John Yes, yes, true, very true. (*To himself, almost*) No, she's been a tower of strength these past few weeks. Don't know what I would have done without her, really. It's been quite ...

Philip (*off*) Sugar?

John Sorry? Oh, yes — two, please — if that's ...

Philip (*off*) Two. And your daughter? Sonia, isn't it?

John Sonia, yes that's right. Good memory for names.

Philip enters with a mug of tea

Philip Goes with the job.

John Of course. Essential. No, Sonia's fine, thanks. Doing very well at university, by all accounts.

Philip Here you go, John. (*He sets the tea down on the table*) Sure you don't want a splash of Scotch in it?

John No thanks, it might curdle the milk.

Philip Come on, get your coat off. Have a seat.

John Yes, right, sure, thanks. (*He takes off his coat, lays it neatly on the bed, and sits at the table*)

Philip You seem a bit edgy.

John Am I? Sorry, Philip.

Philip Relax. You're not here for a job interview.

John No, well, I've been to enough of those over the past few weeks.

Philip Any joy?

John Not really. I am on the shortlist for one. Admin. job — office work, you know — clerical assistant sort of thing.

Philip Tea boy, in other words.

John Well, no not ... It's more ... Look, to be quiet honest, Philip, since that unfortunate business, I can't really afford to be choosy.

Philip Must be difficult for you.

John I must admit, I'm getting quite desperate.

Philip Good — God. It's a terrible state of affairs, isn't it? All your experience and expertise, and you're having to, well, demean yourself like this — and purely because of some minor indiscretion.

John Yes, well ... (*An awkward little pause*) Anyway, how're things with you Philip?

Philip Things? Well, let's see: kicked out of my own house — which I'm still paying for — solicitor's fees escalating daily ——

John Divorce not through yet, then?

Philip Not yet. No, *things* are wonderful, John, just wonderful.

John Sorry, Philip, I shouldn't have ... Still, at least you've got a decent job — that's one up on me, isn't it?

Philip Maybe.

John No, you're doing all right there. As long as you keep hitting those sales targets, eh?

Philip There's one or two still left to hit.

John I really miss it you know — the job. Out on the road, meeting the clients, all the interaction.

Philip (*sarcastically*) Yeah — grin, nod, shake hands, fake sincerity.

John (*missing Philip's sarcasm*) Yes, yes indeed. Sell, sell, sell! That feeling you get when you've made a sale, it's like ——

Philip Prostitution.

John What? Oh, right. Yes ... But, no, I mean, once a salesman, always a salesman, eh?

There is a knock at the door

Philip That'll be Dave.

John Oh, I didn't realize anybody else was coming.

Philip opens the door to Dave. Dave is a few years younger than Philip and is dressed in a smart, fashionable suit; he carries a briefcase and a carrier bag. In contrast to John, he is loud and self-confident

Dave (*singing, badly*) "God rest you merry gentlemen, let nothing you dismay ... !" (*He steps into the room*)

Philip Bit early for carols, Dave.

Dave Only six weeks, mate. Get in first, I say. (*To John*) All right?

Philip This is John.

John (*getting up to shake hands with Dave*) Hallo. Nice to ——

Dave (*walking straight past John*) Jesus, what a craphole. Sorry, Phil, no offence.

Philip None taken.

Dave How much they charging you for this?

Philip Six hundred.

Dave A month?

Philip London prices, Dave.

Dave Yeah, but it ain't exactly Knightsbridge round here, is it? Furnished?

Philip What you see is what you get.

Dave And what you get is shit. Where's your telly?

Philip Don't have one.

Dave You're kiddin'? Six hundred a month, to sit in here, on your own — without a TV? What do you do with yourself? No, don't answer that.

Philip Scotch?

Dave Yeah. That'll do for starters. Got some beers in here (*the carrier bag*) — stick 'em in the fridge, will you? I take it you do have a fridge?

Philip takes the carrier from Dave and exits into the kitchen

Dave dumps his briefcase on the bed and does a little tour of the room, ending up at the cabinet

Six hundred a month for this. He must be barking.
John Well, it's ——
Dave Have you seen the neighbourhood?
John Yes, I ——
Dave Rancid. (*A thought*) Hold on, you don't live round here, do you?
John No.
Dave Thank God for that.
John No, I live out in ——
Dave (*by the cabinet*) Look at this — plastic cups. He must be hard up.

Philip enters. He edges between Dave and the cabinet and pours two cups of Scotch during the following

Was just saying Phil, nice neighbourhood.
Philip A bit grim, isn't it?
Dave Grim? I thought I was gonna get mugged on the way from the station.

Philip holds out a cup to Dave

(*Taking the cup*) Cheers!
Philip Cheers!

John half-heartedly raises his mug

Come straight from work, Dave?
Dave Oh, you can tell, can you?
Philip Nice suit. Expensive?
Dave Well, it weren't second-hand.
Philip Doing well then?
Dave Doing all right. (*He sits at the table opposite John*)
Philip Working hard?
Dave Listen, my boss called me in the other morning: he said, "Dave, please slow down, you're making the rest of the team look bad!" I said, "I'm sorry guv, I don't know how." Hundred and ten per cent, full throttle, no prisoners — it's the only way.
Philip Dave's in Sales.
John Yes, I guessed that. What is it you sell?
Dave Photocopiers.
John Ah.

Dave Kurtis — with a K. German company.

John Sorry, I've not heard of them.

Dave International photocopier of the year two years running.

John Really?

Dave Can't go wrong with a credential like that. It's a gift.

Philip (*sitting at the table*) John used to be a salesman, Dave.

Dave Yeah? All reps together then, eh? What line?

John What line? Oh, stationery — office supplies.

Dave Right — rubber bands and paper clips? Sounds a bit dull. No wonder you jacked it in.

Philip They jacked John in.

Dave What? (*Awkwardly*) Oh, right. Sorry to … That's the trouble with Sales, isn't it? Cut-throat. Don't hit your targets and you're out on your … Can I have another drink, Phil?

Philip Help yourself.

Dave gets up and fixes himself another Scotch

Dave God knows what I'd do if I lost my job, or, more to the point, what the missis would do, eh?

Philip How is Gemma?

Dave Gemma? Oh, you know, still making impossible demands on my body and my bank balance.

Philip High maintenance, eh?

Dave Very. It's like havin' a Ferrari. Lovely to look at, goes like a rocket, but the running costs are astronomical! (*He laughs at his own joke*) Not that I'm complaining. I mean, if you want the best you got to be prepared to pay for it, right? That's my philosophy. You've met her, Phil.

Philip Only briefly.

Dave Wouldn't you say she's worth it?

Philip Yes, she is very …

Dave (*producing his wallet and taking a photo from it*) This is her, John — on the beach in Thailand last summer.

John (*looking at the photo; embarrassed*) Very nice.

Dave puts the photo back in his wallet and sits

Philip I don't know how you manage it, Dave.

Dave Manage what?

Philip Well, exotic holidays, high maintenance wife, the new house. You should see their new house, John — very upmarket. I dread to think what the mortgage is like.

Dave Fat.

Philip Can't be easy, trying to keep up that standard of living.

Dave No. Well ...

Philip Must be a real struggle.

Dave It is — sometimes. But, like I say, I'm not complaining. And at least I'm not forking out six hundred a month for a basement bedsit slum. Come on, Phil, I know the missis kicked you out, but surely you could find yourself something better than this, surely.

Philip I'm not living here.

Dave No?

Philip Course not. No, this *slum* is purely for business.

Dave Business? What sort of business you gonna do in a dump like this?

Philip That's the reason I asked you here, Dave.

Dave Boys' night out, you said.

Philip I know what I said.

Dave Look, Phil, it's Friday night. I came here to get pissed, play cards, and watch some porn, not talk business. I've been talking business all fucking week.

Philip This is different.

Dave Yeah? Some sort of Egyptian bollocks, I s'pose? (*Getting up*) Sorry, I'm not interested.

Philip It's not pyramid selling. Nothing like that, I assure you. Just sit down a minute.

Philip gets up and eases Dave back into his seat. He takes a moment now — this is going to be the biggest sales pitch of his life

Do you think I would ask you here tonight if I didn't think it was worthwhile? Do you think I would even try to talk you into doing anything you didn't want to do? I wouldn't be able to. You're both sales people — you know all the angles. You're both much too smart to fall for any kind of bullshit. And that's the reason I chose you — because you're smart, both of you. All I want you to do is to listen to my proposition, my business plan. Listen, ask questions, and if you don't like what you hear, you can go home to your wives or we can just sit around and get pissed, whatever. Agreed?

John Agreed.

Dave (*shrugging*) Yeah, go on then.

Philip Right, hypothetical question: (*picking up Dave's briefcase*) If you were to find a briefcase containing, say, a thousand pounds, in cash, what would you do?

Dave Easy. Straight down to the casino and put it on thirteen black.

Philip John?

John Well, at this present moment in time it would be tempting to keep the money, I must confess. But no, I'd hand it in to the police.

Philip Why?

John Well, it obviously must belong to someone.

Dave Yeah, well anyone stupid enough to leave a grand in a suitcase lying about deserves to lose it.

John Not necessarily. It might belong to someone old — someone who really needs it.

Philip True. What if it was ten thousand? Fifty? A hundred thousand?

John Well, surely the amount doesn't really matter. It's the principle, isn't it?

Philip One hundred thousand pounds? Are your principles that strong?

John I'd like to think so.

Philip Come on, John. You said yourself, things are tough.

John At the moment.

Philip Going to get tougher. Let's face it, you're not a young man any more, and who's going to want to employ you after what you did?

Dave Why, what did you do?

John Look, do we have to —— ?

Philip Doesn't look too good on your CV, does it? Instant dismissal for dishonesty.

John Philip, please ——

Philip Your principles didn't stop you fiddling your expenses, did they?

A pause

John Thank you, Philip. Yes, I did have a moment of weakness. For which I am ashamed, and regretful of. But, well — all the more reason why I should try to redeem myself now.

Philip With a mortgage to pay, a wife to look after, a daughter at university. Redemption isn't much good to them, is it?

John Can we leave my family out of this, please?

Philip One hundred thousand pounds, John. The answer to all your problems.

John No.

Dave Go on, Johnny, take it mate. I mean, look at it like this: what old or needy person is going to have a hundred grand to lose anyway? Chances are it belongs to some rich bastard, or some drug dealer or something.

Philip Well?

John I don't know.

Dave I bloody do.

Philip You sure, Dave?

Dave Yeah, no worries. Sod principles.

Philip OK. Well, let's introduce a risk element into the scenario.

Dave Fire away.

Philip Let's say that it's stolen money. From, I don't know, a bank robbery.
Dave Well, I'm not going to know that, am I?
Philip Let's say you do. You know exactly where the money has come from.
Dave What, I'm part of the gang, am I?
Philip Not necessarily.
Dave Well, then, how do I get hold of it?
Philip It doesn't matter.
John Perhaps you saw the robbers throw the briefcase away while they were escaping.
Dave Why would they want to do that? Why go to all the trouble of robbing a bank and then just toss away the loot?
John Well, if the police were in hot pursuit …
Dave Then as soon as I pick it up the cops will see me. Surely.
Philip Look, it doesn't really ——
John Not if they threw the case into a rubbish skip, with the intention of returning later to collect it.
Dave Yeah, right. And I saw them do it, then waited till the police went by …
Philip Just shut up a minute! Both of you. Look, it doesn't matter how you came by the money, OK? This is all hypothetical. The important thing is that you have found a hundred thousand pounds of stolen money. What are you going to do?
Dave There's no chance of me getting caught?
Philip Of course there's a chance you'll get caught.
Dave Ah, well — that ups the ante, doesn't it?
Philip A hundred grand, Dave.
Dave Even so — risky.
Philip Come on, Dave. You like to gamble.
Dave Yeah, but ——
Philip I've seen you pumping money into those fruit machines.
Dave That's not illegal.
Philip The dogs, the horses ——
Dave Neither is that.
Philip No, but you do play for some pretty high stakes.
Dave Sometimes.
Philip I mean, some of the stories I've heard …
Dave What stories?
Philip Well, there's the one about you losing a grand in some card game over at ——
Dave Who told you that?
Philip It's true then?
Dave I had a bad run of luck that night, that's all.
John A thousand pounds?

Dave Look, you play the odds, OK? Sometimes you win, sometimes you lose.

Philip But mostly you lose.

Dave No! I won two hundred quid last week. Well, the week before. And anyway, I enjoy it. It's recreational, that's all.

Philip Recreational? Come on, Dave — you gamble because you need the money: high maintenance wife, the mortgage from hell ... Trouble is, the more you gamble, the more you lose, the more money you need. It's a vicious circle.

Dave (*jumping to his feet*) Fuck off! I'm doin' all right, OK? I'm not ... Two years time — max — I'll be UK Sales Manager. No problem. Right? Yeah? Big bucks, bonuses, I'll be quids in.

Philip In two years' time. Maybe. But, right now, with a hundred thousand tucked away in the bank ...

Dave Yeah, and me tucked away in the nick.

Philip But it is worth the gamble, though? Think about it.

A moment

John What about you, Philip? You've obviously given this scenario some consideration. Would you keep the money?

Philip Me? Absolutely. I'd have no qualms — none whatsoever. How else am I going to get off the treadmill? I spend all my energy on a job that just goes round and round in circles, solely to support a failed marriage and a mountain of debts. What sort of existence is that? Well, bollocks to principles, and to hell with the risk; if an opportunity like that came my way I would seize it with both hands. Don't tell me you wouldn't.

Dave OK, maybe you're right. But this is all hypothetical, isn't it? We still haven't heard your proposition.

Philip I'm coming to that. Another drink, anyone?

John Not for me.

Dave Yeah. I'll have a beer.

Philip goes out to the kitchen

Dave takes off his jacket, hangs it on the back of his chair and sits

What d'you reckon, John?

John About what?

Dave What he's driving at?

John I don't know. It's not what I expected.

Dave What isn't?

John Whatever it is he's driving at.

Dave No. Me neither.

Philip enters with a can of lager for Dave

Philip No glasses, I'm afraid. (*He hands Dave the lager and pours himself another Scotch*)
Dave Come on, Phil — shoot.
Philip Mm. I'm not sure.
Dave About what?
Philip I'm just not sure if this is right for you both.
Dave Not right? What d'you mean?
Philip Look, you both obviously need the money, we've established that. But then, who doesn't? It's just that, the sort of money I'm talking about has to be earned. And earning it requires a certain type of person.
Dave And you're saying we're not?
Philip Look, Dave, you've seen these guys — your age, some younger — in their Porsches and Maseratis, all Rolex and Ray-Bans. Smug and smooth and oozing money.
Dave Yeah, I see 'em all the time. Bastards.
Philip Well. They must have something that you don't, surely. Otherwise, you'd be in their position.
Dave Bollocks. They're just lucky, that's all.
Philip Luck? Is that all it is?
Dave Right place at the right time, that's what it's all about.
Philip But more deserving than you?
Dave No way.
Philip John?
John Well, it's not just luck, is it? You can't be a success in any business without hard work, and a certain acumen.
Philip So how come you never made it? After — what was it — twenty-two years in the same company? You weren't even in management.
John No, but ——
Philip Younger men coming in, been with the company five minutes — they're getting pay rises, bonuses, promotion over your head. They must obviously have been smarter, harder-working …
John No, not at all.
Philip More honest though.
John (*angrily and bitterly*) That's not fair! I resent that! Twenty-two years, and I never claimed a penny more than I was entitled to. Not a damn penny! (*He rises*) Everyone else did, I know that. They used to boast about it — bloody wide boys. Boast how much they'd screwed out the company. But not me — not "good old honest John". They used to joke about it behind my back — as if I was some sort of oddball because I was honest.

Sniggering bloody wide boys. Once, only once ... One moment of weakness, and I get caught — sacked — humiliated. It's so unfair, so bloody unfair. (*Suddenly aware of his outburst*) Sorry. I'm sorry.

Philip puts a friendly hand on John's shoulder and sits him back down

Philip Don't apologize, John. I'm not surprised you're bitter. You are an intelligent man, you served your company with diligence — and integrity. And what happens? One mistake and they just toss you out on to the scrapheap. No company car, no pension scheme, no future. And the truth is that the same thing could just as easily happen to any of us.

Dave So what's the answer?

Philip Being in the right place at the right time, you said? That's partly true. But it's not enough just being there, you also have to be prepared to grab and take what it is you want. The only question is; how far will you go to get it?

The question hangs in the air for a moment

Dave You mean stepping outside the law. That's what you're driving at. That's what he's driving at, John.

John Something illegal, you mean?

Philip What's the matter, is the prospect so horrifying?

Dave That depends, doesn't it.

Philip On what? The gravity of the crime? Or whether you can get away with it or not?

John The crime, surely.

Philip Really? How often do you exceed the speed limit, Dave? Or should I say how often do you drive within the speed limit?

Dave Oh, come on, that's not ——

Philip Ton up on the M25 — it's breaking the law. Not only that, but if you lost your licence you could lose your job. A lot at stake.

Dave Yeah, but ——

Philip But you continue to do it because you're fairly sure you can get away with it. Right?

Dave Yeah. I suppose.

Philip John, how did you feel when you were caught fiddling your expenses? Ashamed?

John Yes. Of course. Very.

Philip Would you have felt ashamed if you'd got away with it?

John Well ...

Philip Of course you wouldn't! If you hadn't been caught you'd probably still be doing it. You wouldn't have felt ashamed, you'd have felt quite pleased with yourself — excited even.

John I don't think so.

Philip No? Come on, everybody's at it these days — businessmen, politicians, so-called sportsmen — so why not you? Insider trading, tax evasion, bribes, back handers — it's all outside the law. Makes what you did seem like peanuts.

John But that still doesn't make it right. Does it?

Philip It doesn't matter. That's what I'm trying to say. There is no right or wrong any more — just those who get away with it and those who don't.

A moment

John What is it, Philip? What is it you want us to do?

Philip I just need to take a leak. I'll be back in a sec.

Philip exits into the bathroom

Dave How well d'you know him?

John Philip? Quite well, I suppose. Only through work, really. You know, meet up once a month for lunch — in a pub or a café — talk about this and that, put the world to rights …

Dave Same here. Never gives much away, though, does he?

John He's very deep.

Dave Deep, yeah. He reads the *Guardian*.

John Mmm.

There is the sound of the toilet flushing

Philip enters

Philip Drink, anyone?

John No thanks.

Dave I'm all right.

Philip OK.

Dave Fire away then.

Philip Ten minutes' work, that's all I'm asking. Ten minutes' work for a minimum of one hundred thousand pounds each. In cash.

John I'm not sure I like the sound of this.

Dave Go on. I'm listening.

Philip There's a large department store, just off Bond Street, Jarvis and Klein. You know it?

Dave J and K's. Yeah — big, old-fashioned place. Sort of upmarket Debenhams.

John Gilly and I went there once. We didn't actually buy anything, but we did have a pot of tea and some scones in their restaurant. Quite expensive, as I recall.

Philip It's upmarket, old-fashioned and *everything* is expensive.

Dave So what is it we're meant to do, go on a massive shoplifting spree?

Philip It's very popular with tourists — and with the older generation. Which means that, although most purchases are made by credit card, there are still a significantly high percentage of cash transactions.

John I prefer to pay cash myself, actually. I find that ——

Dave Shut up a minute, John, I've got a feeling we're finally getting to the meat here. Go on, Phil.

Philip The store has thirty-three tills in operation — including the two cafés, and the restaurant. On average each till will take approximately one thousand pounds in cash, in one hour. In the two weeks running up to Christmas you can probably treble that. Which is ...

Dave Ninety-nine K an hour.

Philip Thank you. They're open from nine to six?

John Nine hours. That's ...

Dave Eight hundred and ninety-one grand every day.

Philip In cash alone.

John That's quite a turnover.

Philip The tills are emptied, hourly, on a rota basis, by security staff, and the money taken to the cashier's office on the fifth floor, where it's counted and banked up.

John How do you know all this?

Philip I was in the store one lunchtime, about a year ago. Looking for a Christmas present for my wife, ironically. This was before she kicked me out, of course. The place was packed — heaving with hordes of Hooray Henrys and Henriettas, rich Japs and Yanks and Arabs, all pushing and shoving and spending obscene amounts of money. I was up on the fourth floor, fed up with shopping, and I needed a piss. Looked around for a toilet, couldn't see one.

John I think they're on the second floor, if I remember ——

Philip John.

John Sorry, Philip.

Philip I saw this door marked "Private — Staff Only". I was feeling impatient, getting a bit desperate, so I just went through. Walked down a corridor, then up a flight of stairs, through another door, down another corridor, and eventually I found the staff toilets.

John Didn't anyone see you?

Philip Yes. There was a bloke in there, washing his hands.

John Didn't he say anything?

Philip As I remember he made some quip about the management. I laughed, he laughed, and then he left.

Dave So he just assumed you were a member of staff?

Philip Obviously. I mean, who would dare to venture beyond that most ultimate of security measures — a door marked "Private"?

John Just a minute though, I seem to remember the staff wearing a uniform. Sort of burgundy blazer, with the J and K motif embroidered ...

Philip The shop staff do, yes, but not the office workers. Behind these doors marked "Private" are offices: Customer Services, Accounts, Stock Control, Post Room, and, on the fifth floor, at the end of a corridor, behind an unmarked door, is the Cashier's Office. (*He goes to the cabinet and pours himself a Scotch*) Once a week, over the past year, I've spent an hour or so wandering around the store — on the shop floors and in the corridors and offices out the back. I'm on nodding terms with at least half the staff, conversational with a few — including a couple of security men. I've even made myself an identity tag. (*He shows them a plastic laminated ID card*)

Dave And no-one's twigged you?

Philip No-one.

John I find that astonishing.

Philip This is a big shop, with a lot of very busy staff. Why should anyone be suspicious of me, an unremarkable man in a suit and tie? I don't have a broken nose or tattoos — I don't look like a crook, do I?

Dave No, but you're not though, are you? A crook.

Philip No. And that is exactly why we can get away with it. You see, most major criminals are caught because they *are* criminals. They're known to police, their fingerprints are on record, informants grass them up ——

Dave Hold on. Get away with what, exactly?

Philip downs his Scotch

Philip What are you doing on the tenth of December?

John When?

Philip Friday the tenth of December. Around twelve forty-five.

John I don't have my Filofax with me.

Philip Whatever you're doing, cancel it. We're going shopping.

John Shopping?

Philip At twelve forty-five, on Friday the tenth of December, we are going to walk into Jarvis and Klein's Department Store, and ten minutes later walk out, at least one hundred grand a piece richer.

A moment

Dave This is a wind-up, right?

John What?

Dave He's havin' a laugh, John.

Philip I'm serious.

Dave Course you are.

Philip One hundred thousand pounds. Enough money to liberate you from whatever trap you've found yourself in. The opportunity is there, if you're prepared to take it.

John But — me? Us? I mean, how?

Philip It's really quite simple.

Dave Simple? Come on, Phil, if it's simple why hasn't anybody else done it?

Philip Because nobody else has thought of it.

Dave Oh sure. And you're a criminal mastermind.

Philip You haven't heard my plan yet.

Dave (*shrugging*) What d'you reckon, John? Shall we humour him?

John Well, I suppose …

Philip OK, listen. The beauty of it is that I have already breached their security. I can now roam around the store without being challenged. My face is recognized and accepted.

Dave So this is like an inside job, that isn't?

Philip Yes.

John Because you're not really an insider.

Philip No.

Dave So where do we come in?

Philip Well, most armed robberies require brute force or some skill at opening locks. But you won't need that. My face will open the right doors, and all you'll have to do is ——

Dave Hold on, hold on. You did just say armed robberies?

Philip Yeah.

Dave Armed, as in, like, with guns?

Philip Yeah.

Dave Whoa! That's it! Now I know you're taking the piss.

Philip What's wrong?

Dave What's wrong? What's … ? Are you honestly expecting us to fuck around with guns? You get life for that! At best we'd end up shooting ourselves. No way, matey. (*He gets up*) Come on, John, get your coat, the man is completely off his trolley.

John (*rising*) Yes, I … Sorry, Philip, I've got to agree with Dave on this one.

Dave puts on his jacket, John puts on his coat. Philip goes to the cabinet, opens the drawer and takes out the gun

Philip I'm sorry, but you're not going anywhere.

Dave (*turning to Philip*) Listen, if you think I'm going to stay here and —
— (*He sees Philip pointing the gun and freezes*)

John freezes as well

Philip (*shouting*) Shut up, Dave! Just sit down and shut the fuck up! Now!

Dave sits

(*To John*) You too!

John sits

Do you really think I can just let you walk out of here? After everything I've told you? Do you? (*He sticks the gun right into Dave's face*) Now, you are gonna do exactly what I tell you, right? *Right?*

Dave nods furiously. Philip takes a breath, then steps back and lowers the gun

You see? You see how easy it is? Here, try it. (*He tosses the gun into Dave's lap*)

Dave recoils, but catches the gun

Dave Shit!
Philip It's all right — it's not real.
Dave What?
Philip It's a replica. A good one.
Dave (*with a massive sigh of relief*) Oh … You bastard.
Philip Sorry, Dave. John. Really I am. But you wouldn't have believed me if I'd told you how easy it was. With a gun in your hand and a loud enough voice, you can have complete control of a situation.
John (*still in shock*) You nearly gave me a heart attack.
Philip I've got another one here. (*He goes to the cabinet, takes out another gun and hands it to John*)
John (*holding the gun reluctantly*) No, I don't think …
Philip Come on, John, hold it properly.

John holds the gun as if to fire it

That's it! Now stand up.

Philip pulls John to his feet

There! Now, can't you feel the authority it gives you? No-one's going to snigger at you now, are they?

A moment

Well, what do you reckon?

John stands there, pointing the gun into nowhere. Dave, still seated, looks up and points his gun at Philip

Dave Get me a beer, you bastard.

Philip Beer? Sure. John?

John (*turning and pointing his gun at Philip*) Yes, I think I'll have that drink now, please.

Philip (*putting his hands up*) Anything you say. Beer or Scotch?

John Do you have a sherry at all?

Philip Just beer or Scotch.

John Scotch then. Please. With a splash of water. Thank you.

Philip exits into the kitchen

Dave gets up, stretching himself back into shape. He and John look at each other — brothers in arms

Dave Well, John? Can you see us as Butch and Sundance?

John Who?

Dave Armed robbers? Blaggers?

John Not really, no. Half an hour ago I was talking about getting a job in an office. Now I'm being asked to be a gun-toting desperado. This whole thing is getting beyond me.

Philip enters with Dave's beer

Philip There you go, Sundance.

Dave Cheers.

Philip What's getting beyond you, John?

John The whole concept of — me as a criminal. I just can't, you know, visualize it. I mean, I'm sure you have a plan, which could work, in theory. But in practice? (*He sits and puts the gun on the table*)

Dave Yeah, look ... Of course, we need the money, we're all pretty desperate for it. John tried fiddling his expenses, I try beating the bookie. So yes, we are prepared to go the extra yard to get it. But what you're talking about ... I dunno. It's just too much. (*He sits and puts his gun next to John's*)

Philip OK. Forget the money for a moment. Forget one hundred thousand pounds and what you could do with it. Just answer me this: what have you ever done in your life which has been outstanding? Spectacular? Daring? John?

John Errmm ...

Philip Dave?

Dave Daring? (*He thinks*) I did a bungee jump out in Thailand last summer.

Philip And that's it, is it? Great epitaph: "Here lies Dave Shepherd — once did a bungee jump."

Dave Yeah, OK — so what have you ever done?

Philip Me? Nothing. Big fat zero. I look back on my life, since I left school, and all I see is mediocrity. Mediocre job, mediocre marriage, mediocre lifestyle. Even the word — mediocre — it's so cloying — like some shapeless, grey sludge. And that's been my life — grey and shapeless. Mediocre. Well, that wasn't how it was meant to be, was it? I mean, when you were a kid, you didn't expect it to turn out like that, did you? You wanted to be a daredevil, a secret agent, a racing driver. You were the hero of your own imagination. You knew — just *knew* — that you were going to do something exciting, spectacular with your life. Right?

Dave and John nod — he has them

So what happened? What bloody happened? You got trapped — that's what happened — stuck, waist deep, and slowly sinking in a sludge of mediocrity. Well OK, now I'm throwing you a lifeline, and it's called audacity. Grab a hold of it. Grab a hold, see how good it feels. Audacity! Say it. Say the word.

Dave Audacity.

John Audacity.

Philip Louder.

Dave ⎫ (*together*) Audacity!
John ⎭

Philip Stand up! Shout it!

Dave ⎫ (*together*) Audacity!
John ⎭

Philip There, you see. Just saying the word makes you feel daring and dangerous. Imagine how it would feel to actually do something audacious. Imagine the adrenalin surging through your veins. God, since I came up with this hair-brained scheme I've been revitalized, I've had a thousand volts running through me. OK, we're never gonna be sporting heroes, or film stars, or astronauts, but we have a chance here, maybe our last chance, to do one mad, glorious, audacious thing that we can remember the rest of our lives. Come on Dave, John, what do you say? Are you in?

Black-out

Gillian's and Gemma's homes; areas to either side of the bedsit set

A telephone rings

Two independent spots come up on Gillian and Gemma on either side of the stage, Gemma L, Gillian R, carrying cordless telephones. They're both "at home". Gillian (John's wife) is in her early forties and well-spoken; she's wearing an apron over her Pringle and pearls, and Marigold rubber gloves. Gemma (Dave's wife) is in her late twenties, attractive, tough and streetwise

Gillian removes a glove and answers her phone

Gillian Hallo?

Gemma Who is this please?

Gillian This is Gillian. Who's that?

Gemma Gillian, is it? Well hallo, Gillian, this is Dave's wife, Gemma.

Gillian Dave? Dave who?

Gemma The same Dave that's been ringing you up at least twice a week for the past month.

Gillian I'm sorry, I think you must be mistaken.

Gemma No, I'm not. You see I've got an itemized telephone bill here and your number appears fourteen times. I've checked the dates, and strangely enough these calls all take place on a Monday or Thursday night. The same nights I go out to my aerobics class. Perhaps you'd like to explain?

Gillian Well, he must obviously be calling my husband.

Gemma Your husband?

Gillian John.

Gemma John who?

Gillian John Pearson.

Gemma Never heard of him.

Gillian No, well I must admit I don't ever remember John talking about a Dave.

Gemma Dave Shepherd.

Gillian I'm sorry, no. Did you say Mondays and Thursdays?

Gemma Yeah. Why?

Gillian Well, it's just that I work on Monday and Thursday evenings.

Gemma Do you? Right. Listen — has your husband been behaving strangely, at all?

Gillian John? Behaving strangely? No. Although ...

Gemma What?

Gillian Well, I suppose, he has seemed rather — I don't know — preoccupied just lately.

Gemma Preoccupied?
Gillian Not his usual self.
Gemma Really? Well, I think we need to talk, don't you?

Black-out

SCENE 3

The flat. A week later. About eleven a.m.

Nothing much has changed: the table and chairs have been moved back against the US *wall and there is a new bottle of Scotch on the cabinet*

The Lights come up

Philip (*off*) OK, one last time. Are you ready?
Dave (*off*) Yo!
John (*off*) Just a sec. That's it. Right. Ready.
Philip (*off*) OK, let's go. *One!*
John (*off*) Go through the door marked "Private" ...
Dave (*off*) The job has now begun.

John and Dave enter from the kitchen. They are wearing suits and ties (John's tie is green) and carrying large carrier bags bearing the "J & K" (Jarvis and Klein) motif. They have their guns with them. Philip follows them out

They are all very edgy. Dave and John chant their moves by rote as they mime each action

Philip *Two!*
Dave Walk calmly down the corridor ——
John — till we find the gents' loo.
Philip *Three!*
John Put on coats, gloves and masks ——
Dave — as quick as we can be.

Dave and John produce raincoats, gloves and woollen ski masks from the carrier bags and struggle to put them on as fast as they can during the following

Philip (*timing them*) Come on, you've got thirty seconds for this. Faster!
John Bloody gloves!
Philip Twenty seconds!
Dave All right, all right ...

Once they have got everything on they take a large canvas holdall out of one of the bags

Philip OK. And *four!*
Dave Once the coast is clear ——
John —— make our way to the cashier's door.

They walk to an imaginary door

Philip *Five!*
John Phil knocks on the door ——
Dave —— we duck down and hide.
Philip *Six!*
John As soon as the door opens ——
Dave —— we go in double quick.

They step through the "door"

Philip *Seven!*
John Shut the door behind us ——
Dave —— with our guns at the ready!
Philip And — *go!*

Dave rushes to one end of the room, pointing his gun

Dave (*in a bad Irish accent*) Stand up, put your hands in the air! All of you! Now! Do it! Do it! Come on!
John (*holding his gun to Philip's head*) Right, yes, OK. You — fill up the bags. With money. And … And … (*He sneezes*) Sorry.
Philip OK, stop a minute.

John takes off his mask and blows his nose

Dave Brilliant, Johnny. That's really gonna scare them, isn't it? "Nobody move or I'll sneeze all over you."
John (*angrily*) It's not my fault — it's this mask!
Dave All right, all right. Easy. Calm down.
John Sorry. I think I've got a cold coming. Sorry, Philip.
Philip It's just nerves. The adrenalin will put a stop to that. But you've got to be more aggressive, John — louder, nastier. Show him, Dave.

Dave grabs Philip in a neck hold with his gun to Philip's head

Dave (*in a bad American accent*) Fill the bags, motherfucker! Move it, or die!

John Is that sort of language really necessary?

Philip Yes, it is — or something along those lines. But without the American accent.

Dave I thought it was good.

Philip It was crap. And what was the one you were doing before?

Dave Irish.

Philip Sounded like Long John Silver. Forget it.

Dave Just trying to disguise my voice.

Philip Just stick to what we've rehearsed. No ad libs, all right?

Dave Sorry.

John Sorry, Philip.

Philip In just over an hour's time we're going to be doing this for real. This is your last chance to get it right. So please concentrate. OK, so Dave's covering from the far end of the office, John's by the door, and I'm running round putting cash into the bags. Oh, and don't be alarmed if you see blood dripping from my mouth — it's just fake, theatrical stuff.

Dave Nice one.

Philip Now remember it's a very long narrow office so make sure your eyes and your guns cover everyone. Right, so you give me thirty seconds to grab what I can from off the desks, then … ?

John Yes, it's me, isn't it? (*To an imaginary cashier*) OK, empty the safe, you …

Dave Scumbag!

John (*with difficulty*) You scumbag.

Philip And if the safe is locked?

Dave (*grabbing Philip*) If this safe isn't opened in five seconds I'll blow his fuckin' brains out! One, two …

Philip (*acting*) Please, please!

Dave Three, four …

Philip OK, safe open. You get me to empty it. Then …

John (*to Philip*) Right, you're coming with us.

Philip No.

John No?

Philip No. I'm staying here.

John Sorry?

Philip No, John, I'm acting. I'm saying I don't want to go, so that you have to make me.

John Of course. Yes. (*He gives Philip a pathetic little punch in the stomach*)

Philip Harder, John. Make it look real.

John I can't. I'm sorry. I just don't like all this violence.

Philip What violence? What violence, John? That is the whole point of using me as the hostage. So nobody gets hurt.

John Yes. I know, I know. Look, I'm just nervous, I suppose.

Dave (*taking off his mask*) Listen, Johnny — John — we're all nervous. I'm wound up like a clockwork thing. Like Phil says, it's the adrenalin. It's good for you.

John No, it's not adrenalin. I'm just plain scared.

Philip Of what?

John Of messing it all up.

Philip You are not going to mess anything up. Just follow the plan.

John But what if *they* don't — follow the plan? What if we're challenged out in the corridor? What if they don't open the door to you? What if they set off some sort of hidden alarm? What if ——?

Philip (*exploding*) Christ! How many times have we been over this? Eh? How many times in the past five weeks have we been through all this? It should be fixed — up here — in your head.

John Sorry, Philip. Sorry.

Philip (*calming down*) One more time. Just to be clear. If anything goes wrong up until the point that I knock on the door, then we abort the mission. Turn around, walk out and go home — no richer, but at least having tried.

John Right.

Philip But once that door does open, then we are committed. No turning back. If they do manage to trigger an alarm it will take their lumbering security men at least three minutes to respond. So, we are in and out of there in ...

John In two minutes.

Philip Maximum.

John Right.

Philip Just stay focussed, John. You'll be fine. OK, so where were we ... ?

A mobile phone — with a novelty ring tone — goes off. It's Dave's

Dave Shit.

Philip I don't believe this. (*He pulls out one of the chairs and sits down, head in hands*)

Dave (*answering the phone*) Hi, babe. (*He mouths "Gemma" to John*) No, I'm with a client at the moment. ... No, I can't. ... Look, I'll call you later OK? ... This afternoon, yeah? ... Bye. (*He hangs up*) I'll turn it off.

Dave and John look over at Philip — still with his head in his hands. John, with new-found resolve, goes over and pulls Philip to his feet

John Right — come on, you're coming with us.

Dave gets back into position — pointing his gun

Dave If anyone tries to follow us he's fuckin' dead, all right?
John OK, so: *eight!*
Dave Shut the door behind us ... (*He mimes shutting the "door"*)
John Before we make our escape.
Dave *Nine!*
John Guns, coats, gloves and masks ...
Dave Back into the bags from Jarvis and Klein.

Dave and John remove their coats, gloves, masks and put them into the carrier bags. Philip watches them — his faith in them gradually returning

John And *ten!*
Dave Walk calmly away from the scene ——
John — and back out the way we came in.

They walk towards the kitchen door. Then turn back

Philip OK. That's good. Then what?
John Once we get back out on the shop floor we walk quickly ——
Dave — but calmly ——
John — to the escalator.
Dave I peel off at the third floor and take the stairs the rest of the way.
John Then I do the same on the second floor.
Philip And I ride the escalator all the way down to the ground floor. Remember to keep your heads down. There are security cameras, but they're there to detect shoplifters. All they'll see of you is an unremarkable man in a suit, out doing his Christmas shopping with the rest of the crowd. Then?
John We all use different exits out of the store on to the street and then make our way to the tube station.
Dave Where our getaway train will be waiting.
Philip And straight back here. We may get separated so I'll leave the key on a piece of string through the letter box. Whoever gets back here first can let themselves in. (*He goes to the front door. He produces a key on a piece of string, and attaches the string to a hook next to the letterbox*)

Dave and John put down their bags and move the table and chairs back into the centre of the room

Dave Right. And then ...
Philip We count and divide the money.
John The loot.
Dave One hundred K, each.

Philip At least.

Dave and John sit

Dave What are you gonna do with yours then, Johnny?

John The first thing I shall do, the very first thing, is take Gilly away on a damn good holiday. She deserves that. A cruise, perhaps.

Dave Nice one. Where you gonna say you got the money from?

John I don't know yet — hadn't thought that far ahead.

Dave Lottery. That's what I'm gonna say.

John But I don't do the lottery.

Dave (*giving John a look*) Duh!

John Oh, I see. I don't know if I can lie to Gilly, just like that. I've found it hard enough over the past few weeks, keeping all this a secret from her.

Dave Tell me about it. Gemma's only got to look at me and I feel guilty — and I haven't even done anything yet. She has a highly suspicious nature, does Gemma.

Philip She doesn't suspect anything about this, does she?

Dave No, no, no. Not a thing. I've been too careful for that.

Philip John?

John I don't think so. But she keeps asking me if I'm all right all the time. Wants to know where I'm going, what I'm doing, who I'm seeing.

Philip You haven't mentioned me or Dave?

John No, of course not. I just feel ... Well, it's like being unfaithful.

Dave Yeah. I know what you mean.

John Not that I have been unfaithful.

Dave No, me neither. Not to Gemma. Never. Think about it occasionally. Wouldn't be human if I didn't. But, no, I love her too much, I suppose. Besides, she'd know. She'd suss me out straight away.

John What would she do if she found out about this?

Dave She'd have my balls hanging from the Christmas tree.

John I don't think Gillian would be best pleased either.

Dave Still, it's them we're doing it for, eh?

John Yes, that's right.

Dave Phil's the lucky one. He's gonna have all that dosh to himself. Eh, Phil?

Philip What's that?

Dave You still with us?

Philip Yeah, sorry.

John Anything wrong at all?

Philip No. It's just ... Well, it's not a plan any more, is it? It's a reality. We're actually going through with it. This time tomorrow we could be very rich. Or we could be in Parkhurst.

A moment, as they all consider the weight of this

Dave The way I look at it is this: it's a gamble, right? Odds stacked in our favour, OK — but there could be a joker or two in the pack. Is the prize worth the risk? Yes, definitely. Is the penalty — i.e. imprisonment — worth risking? Again, I think so. And the reason is this: if the wheels do fall off this thing — if it all goes pear-shaped and we get nicked ——

John You don't think we will, do you?

Dave No, no. It's a brilliant plan. It's practically foolproof — provided Phil's done his homework. But, even if we do get caught, we're not going to get massive sentences, are we? Not for first time offenders. And with good behaviour we'd get out on probation in a year or two. And then, right — and this is the brilliant bit — we sell our story to the press! (*He rises; quite animatedly*) Think about it — a story like that would fetch thousands in the tabloids.

John That's very true.

Dave We'd be quids in! We could even write a book about it — "How We Done It" — guaranteed bestseller. They'd probably make it into a film. Think about that, eh? Brad Pitt as Dave Shepherd!

John He's an American, isn't he?

Dave So what? Who'd play you then?

John Oh, I don't know. I don't go to the cinema much these days.

Dave Gandhi.

John What?

Dave The bloke who played Gandhi — in the film. What's his name? You know.

John Oh yes. I like him.

Dave Yeah, he could do you. And Phil … ?

Philip Probably some balding ex-popstar.

Dave But you see my point? Even if we lose, we win. I mean, it's almost worth getting caught for, isn't it?

Philip and John give Dave a look

That's the way I'm looking at it, anyway.

Philip John?

John Me? Oh, I don't think a day's gone past when I haven't thought about backing out. I've hardly slept this past week. This whole thing is wrong and stupid and my instincts are telling me to run away from it all. But run away to what? No, you were right, Philip. If you want something these days, you've got to be prepared to be a bit ruthless to get it. And, well, I'm prepared. (*He rises*)

They stand firm together now: the "Three Musketeers"

Dave You're right — it is stupid.

John Ludicrous, really.
Philip Utter madness.
Dave Well ...
Philip I suppose we'd better ...
Dave Yep.
John (*checking his watch*) It's time.
Philip Oh yes, one last thing before we go: all personal items — wrist-watches, rings, wallets, anything that could be dropped, or identified — leave them here.

Dave and John remove the said items and place them on the table

And the phone, Dave.
Dave (*bringing out and laying down his mobile phone*) Force of habit. Never go anywhere without it.
John Will it be safe to leave all this stuff lying about in here?
Dave Yeah. I mean, there's a lot of thieves about, aren't there?
Philip I'll put them away, out of sight. (*He puts all their stuff away in a drawer in the cabinet*) Check we've got everything — bags, coats, masks, guns ...
Dave Shooters.
Philip All right Dave, shooters.
Dave Check.
John Check.
Philip Good. How about a drop of Dutch courage, before we ... ?
Dave Yeah. Why not?

Philip pours three shots of Scotch and hands them out

John Good luck, Philip, Dave.
Dave Yeah, and you mate. See you in Parkhurst, eh?
Philip Parkhurst!
John Parkhurst!

They down their drinks in one, take a deep breath and exit

A few moments pass, then we hear footsteps coming down the steps to the front door. There is a knock. A pause. Then another knock

Gemma (*off*) Look through the letter box.
Gillian (*off*) Certainly not.
Gemma (*off*) For God's sake — out the way.

The letter box flap goes up, and Gemma peers in

No-one there. Hold on, there's something … (*She pulls through the key on the string and unlocks the door*)

Gemma and Gillian step inside the flat

Gillian Hallo? Is anybody there?
Gemma God what a dump.
Gillian So Gemma, what do we do now?
Gemma We wait Gillian. We wait.

Music

The Lights slowly fade to Black-out

ACT II
Scene 1

The flat. Two minutes later

The Lights come up. As the scene progresses, the Light outside fades to a state suggesting rain

Gemma is alone, taking in her surroundings

Gillian enters from the kitchen. She is quite anxious

Gemma Anything?

Gillian No. A kitchenette, and a bathroom — tiny, and rather unsavoury-looking.

Gemma The whole place is a dump. Not fit for a cockroach.

Gillian I feel very uneasy about this. We're trespassing. It could even be construed as breaking and entering.

Gemma Bloody freezing. (*She goes to the radiator*) D'you know how to work these things?

Gillian Somebody might come back and find us here.

Gemma Well, I bloody hope so. I didn't intend waiting here for nothing.

Gillian Are you sure this is the right place?

Gemma Positive. I watched them go down the steps. And it's the same address I found written in Dave's Filofax.

Gillian So where are they now, then?

Gemma How should I know? They must have left when I went to meet you at the station.

Gillian Well, if they've gone then there's no point in staying here.

Gemma The point, Gillian, is to find out what our husbands are up to.

Gillian You don't know for certain that it *was* my husband you saw.

Gemma Grey hair, grey suit, green tie.

Gillian That could be anyone. Besides, he told me he was going for a job interview this morning.

Gemma Yeah, and Dave told me he was going Christmas shopping this lunchtime. Even had it written down in his diary — followed by a row of exclamation marks.

Gillian And that's why you decided to follow him, is it?

Gemma I could tell he was up to something — I can read him like a book. Anyway, I rang him, didn't I? While he was here — and he told me he was with a client.

Gillian Well, perhaps he was.

Gemma What, in a dump like this?

Gillian Yes, well, I'm sorry, Gemma, I don't know what it is your husband is *up to*, but I'm sure it has nothing to do with my John.

Gemma The secret phone calls — the strange behaviour — the fact that they're both out on the same nights?

Gillian That still doesn't prove that John has ever been *here* though, does it?

Gemma No, but if you'd done what I told you and gone through his pockets and stuff, I'm damn sure you'd have found this address written down somewhere.

Gillian Well I didn't. I wouldn't.

Gemma Why not? Scared of what you might find?

Gillian When you trust someone Gemma, you tend *not* to go through their pockets, their diary. Or go following them through the streets when they leave home in the morning.

Gemma OK. So what are you doing here?

Gillian Pardon?

Gemma If you trust your husband so much, then what are you doing here?

Gillian I'm here because ...

Gemma Well?

Gillian Because — he was wearing the wrong suit.

Gemma What?

Gillian He wasn't wearing his interview suit. John is such a creature of habit, you see. He always wears the same suit and tie for interviews.

Gemma But not today.

Gillian No.

Gemma There you go then. (*She moves to the cabinet and starts opening the drawers*)

During the following, we hear the sound of rain, slowly building in volume

Gillian It's not just that. I thought John might be in some sort of trouble — that's why I came. But I really don't feel comfortable staying here. I'm sorry, Gemma, I've got to go. (*She moves towards the door*)

Gemma Hold on, Gillian. Take a look at this. (*She takes the rings, watches, wallets, etc. from the cabinet and puts them on the table*)

Gillian John's watch. And his ring — his wedding ring.

Gemma And Dave's. And his mobile. Now, he never goes anywhere without that.

Gillian I don't understand. It doesn't make sense.

Gemma Well, it proves they've both been here, doesn't it?

Gillian Yes. I suppose it does. (*She sits*)

Gemma I thought you were going?

Gillian Why would he take off his wedding ring?

Gemma (*sarcastically*) Well, perhaps it was so nobody would know they were married.

Gillian But why should … ? Oh, I see. You think it's that, then?

Gemma Have you got a better explanation?

Gillian Not at the moment, but … Well, you don't know John. He's not the type to go chasing after other women.

Gemma Really? Well maybe they came chasing after him?

Gillian No, not John.

Gemma Why, what's the matter with him?

Gillian Nothing. Nothing's the matter with him at all.

Gemma The only thing I can't work out is this place. No TV. Bare mattress. There can't be anybody actually living here. And why leave all this other stuff behind? (*She picks up John's wallet and begins looking through it*)

Gillian What are you doing? That's John's wallet.

Gemma You look then.

Gillian (*taking the wallet*) What am I supposed to be looking for?

Gemma Clues. Anything. Receipts, notes, names, numbers.

Gillian You're quite enjoying this, aren't you?

Gemma Eh?

Gillian Playing the detective.

Gemma What's that supposed to mean?

Gillian You seem to be quite eager to find some sort of — I don't know — incriminating evidence. It's almost as if you want them to be guilty of something.

Gemma (*picking up Dave's wallet*) Look, you can walk around with your head up your arse and pretend everything's peachy, if you like, but I want to know what's going on. OK?

Gillian Well, you're out of luck, I'm afraid. No receipts, no secret coded messages, just his credit cards, some cash. And some photographs.

Gemma Photographs of who?

Gillian Just some old snaps. I didn't know he kept this one.

Gemma What is it?

Gillian Our honeymoon. In Littlehampton. (*She passes a photo to Gemma*)

Gemma Very nice. Who's the little girl?

Gillian Our daughter, Sonia.

Gemma You took her on your honeymoon?

Gillian John isn't Sonia's natural father.

Gemma Oh. (*She hands the photo back*)

Gillian We had a wonderful time, the three of us.

Gemma Yeah, looks like you're having fun. How long ago was that?

Gillian Fifteen years. Sixteen in April. Sonia's at university now.

Gemma You must've been quite young when you had her.

Gillian Thank you. Yes, I was. Young, and badly married. Her father, her real father, was — well, he was a mistake.

Gemma takes a photo from Dave's wallet and sits

Gemma Look at this. That's me, topless in Thailand.
Gillian Oh.
Gemma Typical of Dave to carry this one around with him. Bet he shows it to all his mates. And all his clients.
Gillian He wouldn't do that, would he?
Gemma You don't know Dave. "Look, that's my wife, that is. See those tits, they belong to me, they do." I'm surprised he doesn't carry a picture of the house round with him, and his car. God, it's cold in here.
Gillian (*rising*) Do you want a cup of tea? There's a kettle and some milk in the kitchen.
Gemma I'll have a coffee — if there's any out there. Black, no sugar. Ta.

Gillian exits into the kitchen

Gemma gets up and goes to the window

Gillian (*off*) What does he do?
Gemma What?
Gillian (*off*) Dave — what does he do? For a job?
Gemma Salesman. He sells photocopiers.
Gillian (*off*) Really? John was a sales rep. Stationery — office supplies. What territory does he cover?
Gemma Territory? I dunno — all over. London, Essex, Kent, Surrey …

Gillian enters, standing in the doorway

Gillian M25 orbital. Same as John.
Gemma That's probably how they met — out on the road, in some greasy spoon café somewhere.
Gillian More likely to be in a Little Chef. John likes Little Chefs.
Gemma Does he? Well, whatever turns you on.
Gillian What? Oh, I see — likes Little Chefs. No, not John. Although …
Gemma What?
Gillian Well, it might explain this flat, the strange behaviour, the secret phone calls to each other.
Gemma I don't follow you.
Gillian Well, you seem convinced there are other women involved.
Gemma Yeah.
Gillian Had it occurred to you that it might not be women?
Gemma What, my Dave and your John … ?
Gillian Homosexual affairs are quite common amongst married men. I was reading a magazine article about it.

Gemma You're serious?
Gillian No. Of course not.

Gillian goes back into the kitchen

*Gemma walks over to the cabinet, picks up the Scotch bottle and the plastic
cups and brings them over to the table*

Gillian enters with two mugs

They both sit down

Coffee. Black, no sugar.
Gemma Ta. Look at this.
Gillian (*sniffing the plastic cups*) Whisky.
Gemma Three of them. So who had the third one?
Gillian Somebody else, I suppose.
Gemma Obviously. But who?
Gillian The third man? A bit like a film, isn't it?
Gemma What film?
Gillian *The Third Man.*
Gemma How d'you know it was a man?
Gillian Whisky — it's a man's drink, isn't it?

*Gemma pours a drop of Scotch into her coffee and offers some to Gillian, who
declines*

So, how long are we supposed to wait?
Gemma Long as it takes. Why? You got to be somewhere?
Gillian Well, I should be at work this afternoon. At the local library. It's just
part-time, but ——
Gemma Phone in sick. That's what I did.
Gillian Where do you work?
Gemma Hairdressers. When I can be bothered.
Gillian Oh.
Gemma I thought you said you had an evening job?
Gillian I do. Just two nights a week. At Tesco's — stacking shelves.
Gemma Really? You don't seem like the shelf-stacking type.
Gillian No? Well, I didn't see myself in that role either, until recently. But
needs must. Since John lost his job we've really needed the extra money.
Actually it's not unbearable, the shelf-stacking. Many different types of
people do it. You'd be surprised.
Gemma I'm sure I would.

Gillian gets up, goes to the window and looks out

Gillian What are we meant to do when they do return?
Gemma Depends.
Gillian On what?
Gemma On who they're with.
Gillian What? Oh God, I hadn't thought of that. You don't think they'd ...
How embarrassing. Oh, this is just awful.
Gemma It will be — for them.
Gillian I don't know how you can stay so calm.
Gemma Calm before the storm, Gillian. Just wait till they walk through that
door.
Gillian Has he — Dave — ever done this sort of thing before?
Gemma What, cheated on me? Not that I know of. It's funny — I've always
known he was a prat, but I never thought he'd do this to me.
Gillian (*sitting down*) I hope you don't mind me asking, but if you've always
known he was ...
Gemma A prat.
Gillian Then why did you ... ?
Gemma Why did I marry him? Good question. He wore me down, I suppose.
Used to come into the salon twice a week for a haircut. He'd sit down and
wouldn't stop talking. He was funny — quite dynamic, in his own way.
Ambitious. I liked that. Seemed determined to actually do something, go
somewhere — instead of just sitting around waiting for things to happen.
Gillian What did happen?
Gemma It was all just bullshit. I suppose I should've seen through it, but
well, he is a salesman, after all. I should've read the small print.
Gillian It's funny, isn't it?
Gemma What is?
Gillian Well, John's not like that at all. Very little ambition, or determination.
Far too modest for his own good. Quite the opposite of your husband. And
yet here we both are, well, in the same boat.
Gemma Yeah, well that just goes to prove, doesn't it? That they're all liars,
they're all full of crap, and sooner or later they always let you down.
Gillian That's very harsh, Gemma.
Gemma It may be very harsh, Gillian, but it's true.
Gillian No. I'm sorry — not John. He may have his faults, but he has never
let us down. Never.
Gemma Oh, well, aren't you the lucky one — married to a saint.
Gillian I didn't say ...
Gemma So where is he now then, eh? What's Saint John up to at this very
moment, do you reckon? Spreading goodwill amongst his fellow man? Or
spreading the legs of another woman? (*Pause*) Sorry.

A moment

Gillian John is a very decent man. Yes, you can sneer at that — it's quite an old-fashioned concept, decency. He's always been very thoughtful, very caring, very dependable. Everything he's done, he's done for me and Sonia. His loyalty to us is beyond question.

Gemma Sounds like there's a "but" coming up.

Gillian But — I haven't always been — as loyal to him.

Gemma What?

Gillian I haven't been completely faithful to John.

Gemma What does "not completely faithful" mean, exactly?

Gillian There have been, during the course of our marriage, affairs.

Gemma Affairs? Affairs — as in more than one?

Gillian Only two.

Gemma Only.

Gillian Two in fifteen years. Just flings. Very brief, very inconsequential.

Gemma Even so. Well, what can I say?

Gillian I don't feel guilty about them. They both just happened.

Gemma This wasn't at the library, was it?

Gillian No. Why?

Gemma Just a mental picture, that's all. Doesn't matter. Carry on.

Gillian There was never a chance John would find out about them. Or even suspect. You are the only person who knows. They served a function — they fulfilled a particular need, at a particular time. That's all. No-one was hurt by them.

Gemma Look, you don't have to justify yourself to me.

Gillian I'm not trying to justify myself to anyone. What I am trying to say is: if John is seeing another woman, if that is what he's doing now, then how could I possibly stand here and judge him? Condemn him? I couldn't, could I?

Gemma No. I suppose not. Well, you're full of surprises, aren't you?

Gillian (*getting up*) Not really, no. But I really think it would be best if I went home. If John wants to talk to me about this, he will — eventually. I'll cross that bridge then. Are you ... ?

Gemma I'm staying right here. You see, I don't like being deceived. I don't think it's very — decent. And when my darling husband comes through that door I won't have no conscience about ripping him into little shreds. Any message you want me to pass on to yours?

Gillian No. You won't say anything about ... ?

Gemma None of my business, is it?

Gillian Thank you. (*She looks out of the window*) God, it's pouring down out there now.

Gemma You'd better ring for a cab.

Gillian I don't have a phone.
Gemma Here, use this. (*She picks up Dave's phone and hands it to Gillian*)
Gillian Is it all right to use this ... ?
Gemma Fine by me. Not my phone.
Gillian Right. Do you know any numbers?
Gemma Oh, give it here. (*She takes the phone back and taps in a number*)

There is the sound of footsteps outside

Gillian What's that?
Gemma What? Oh shit! In here — quick!

Gemma ushers Gillian into the kitchen, then remembers the rings, watches, etc. on the table. She scoops them up quickly

A hand reaches through the letter box for the key

Gemma dives into the kitchen

The front door opens and Dave and Philip come tumbling in. Both are rain-soaked and breathless. Dave is clutching one of the Jarvis and Klein carriers, which he puts down on the table. Philip stays by the door, checking to see if they have been followed

Dave (*between breaths*) Is there — anyone — out there?
Philip No-one. It's OK.
Dave Thank God.

Philip shuts the door

Philip What did you start running for?
Dave I dunno. I thought ... I'm sure I was being followed.
Philip That was me.
Dave No. On the tube. When I got off the train. I'm sure ...
Philip There was no-one. You're being paranoid.
Dave Sorry. Shit, Phil. Fuck! Oh, fuckin' fuck! Shit!
Philip Calm down. Get a hold of yourself. Deep breaths.
Dave Yeah. Yeah. Right. (*He breathes deeply*)
Philip Better?
Dave No.
Philip What happened to John?
Dave What happened to John? What d'you mean what happened? You were there — you saw him. He lost it, went nuts ...

Philip No, afterwards — outside. Did you see where he went?

Dave No. Just took off. On his toes. Don't know where.

Philip Shit.

Dave They'll have caught him. They'll have caught him and he'll blab. He'll tell them everything. They'll be on the way here now. We gotta go. We gotta get out of here! (*He makes for the door*)

Philip blocks Dave, pushes him back

Philip We're going nowhere. We stay put until John gets here. OK? *OK?*

Dave All right. (*He calms down*) Sorry, Phil.

Philip Did he have the bag with him? The last time you saw him, did he still have the bag?

Dave Yeah. I think so.

Philip Good.

There is a moment, as they gather their thoughts

Dave We did it, Phil.

Philip Yeah.

Dave We actually did it.

Philip I know …

Dave I can't believe it. I mean — shit — you know, we actually …

Philip Did it. Yeah. But let's not break out the champagne just yet.

Dave I feel sick.

Dave rushes off to the bathroom — and we hear him throwing up

Philip picks up the bottle of Scotch and the cups from the table. He looks puzzled for a moment, then places them back on the cabinet

The toilet flushes

Dave enters

Dave Sorry.

Philip It's all right. Feel better now?

Dave Yeah. Just a bit too much adrenalin, that's all.

Philip Sure.

Dave Any sign of him?

Philip No.

Dave Where d'you think he went?

Philip I don't know. He looked …

Dave Mental. His eyes! Did you see them? What was he on?

Philip Adrenalin.
Dave Look, I need a glass of water. You want one?
Philip No.
Dave Tea? Coffee?
Philip No.
Dave Sure?
Philip Yeah.
Dave You know, I still can't believe we actually did it.

Dave exits into the kitchen. A second later we hear him cry out in shock.
He backs out, straight into Philip, followed by Gemma and Gillian

Gemma What, Dave? What is it you can't believe you actually did?
Dave Gemma?
Gemma You seem surprised to see me.
Dave Uh ... ?
Philip Dave?
Gemma Oh, pardon me. We haven't been introduced. Come on, Dave, introduce me to your friend.
Dave What? Oh — um — Phil. This is Gem ... Gemma. My, erm ...
Gemma His wife.
Philip (*trying to stay calm*) I know. We've met.
Gemma Have we?
Philip Briefly. Your housewarming party, last ——
Gemma Really? Well, Philip, sorry I don't remember you. Now, perhaps you would like to tell me *what the bloody hell is going on?!*
Gillian (*stepping forward*) Where's John? What's happened to him. Is he all right?
Philip John? You must be Gillian.
Gillian Yes. You must be the third man. Where's John?
Philip I ... I'm afraid we're not too sure. We got separated. Sorry, can I ask you what you're both doing here?
Gemma No, you can't. We're asking the questions, and you better start answering.
Dave I need to go to the toilet ...
Gemma Stay where you are! Well? I'm waiting.

Dave and Philip look to each other for inspiration. Dave gets it first

Dave Christmas shopping.
Gemma What?
Dave We've been Christmas shopping — haven't we, Phil? Christmas shopping — for presents — for you, and for her, and ... It was a surprise thing — we didn't want you to know. And that's why we ... That's why ...

Gemma That's why you've been sneaking about for the past six weeks. That's why you've been meeting in this craphole, is it? Well, how sweet of you. Isn't that nice of them, Gillian? OK, so what have you got us then? Let's have a look. (*She moves towards the J&K carrier on the table*)

Dave blocks Gemma

Dave No! You can't. You'll spoil the surprise. It's ...
Philip (*shaking his head*) Dave.

Dave reluctantly moves aside

Gemma (*delving into the carrier*) Jarvis and Klein? Very tasteful. Not like you, Dave. Now let's see what you've bought us. Well, how lovely. You've bought us an old raincoat — a man's raincoat. And some gloves ...
Dave Gemma.
Gemma And ... (*She takes out the gun*) What the fuck ... ?!
Gillian Oh my God!
Dave It's all right. It's not real.

There is a sudden, urgent knocking at the door. They all freeze for a second, then Philip checks through the window and opens the door

John — in his raincoat — falls inside, clutching the holdall. Philip catches him

Gillian John!

Black-out

SCENE 2

The same. A few minutes later

The Lights come up. It seems darker outside now, and the light bulb is on; the sound of rain continues. During the following, the sound of the rain fades away

John sits at the table, with his coat off, his tie loose, and his head in his hands. Dave sits on the other side of the table. Philip stands to one side of the table, Gemma on the other. In the centre of the table are the holdall and the gun

Gillian enters from the kitchen carrying a mug of tea, which she sets down on the table in front of John

Gillian Here. A cup of tea, John.
John (*looking up, sheepishly*) Thanks. (*He takes a sip of tea*)

Everyone watches John in anticipation. Eventually he summons up a voice

(*Wearily and confusedly*) I don't really know what happened. Everything was going just as we'd planned — just like clockwork. Almost as if it wasn't really me doing it — like I was on autopilot or something. I could hear myself shouting, but it didn't sound like my voice. Shouting and pointing the gun ... There was this chap — I think he must have been the manager or supervisor or something. I had the gun pointed at him — right in his face — and I told him to open the safe. *"Open the safe."* So why wouldn't he do it? Why wouldn't he open the bloody safe? "No." That's all he said, nothing else, just "No." He had this look in his eyes — so stubborn, so arrogant — and I felt so angry with him. I mean, it wasn't his money, was it? Why should he stick his neck out like that? Stupid, stupid man. (*Pause*) I don't remember hitting him. But if you say I did I suppose I must have done. All I remember was that suddenly everything was so real and happening so quickly. I just wanted to get out of there, as quick as I could. I panicked — I ran. (*To Dave*) Was he all right? The man, was he all right?
Dave He was conscious. But he was bleeding a lot, from the side of his head. You must have caught him with the gun.
John (*distraught*) No. Oh, no.
Philip What happened then, John? When you got outside.
John I was disorientated — couldn't think. Then I saw this door — fire exit — went through it — down the stairs. They seemed to go on forever.
Philip Did you pass anyone?
John No. I don't think so. I may have done. It's all a blur, really. Until I got outside, and the cold air and daylight hit me. There were crowds of people everywhere, Christmas shoppers — hordes of them. Seemed like they were all coming towards me. So I started to run again — just kept running. I thought I was going to have a heart attack. (*Pause*) Found myself in the park — Hyde Park — near the boating lake. Alone. Sat on a bench — trying to catch my breath, gather my thoughts. Then I realized I still had the bag, and the gun. I was going to throw them both in the lake, but I thought someone might see me. So I left the park, got a bus part of the way, then walked the rest. But, as I did, the panic started to build again — it seemed there were policemen everywhere I looked. I started to run again — ran all the way here. I don't know if they saw me. They might have followed me here. I don't know. I ...

Dave Shit. (*He gets up and rushes to the window*)

John I'm sorry. I've let you down. I've let you all down.

Philip No, you haven't, John. You're here, you're safe. That's the main thing.

John Gilly, I'm so ... (*He turns to Gillian*)

Gillian hesitates for a moment, but he seems so forlorn ...

Gillian (*putting her hands on his shoulders*) It's all right, dear. It's all right.

Gemma (*not so sympathetic*) All right? Are you serious? These utter wankers commit armed robbery — with violence — and you say it's all right?

Gillian I didn't say what they did was all right. I just meant ——

Gemma What possessed you, eh? What got into your bloody stupid minds? You're gonna have to tell me, because I am having real problems just trying to comprehend what you've done. Well, come on. I'm waiting.

The three men hang their heads like naughty schoolboys

Dave (*mumbling*) It was just ... Well ...

Gemma Can't hear you.

Dave We were desperate. We needed the money and ——

Gemma So does everybody else. But not everybody goes out and robs a West End department store to get it, do they? And why not? Because they're not bloody stupid, that's why not.

Dave But we got away with it.

Gemma What does that matter? The fact is, you risked getting caught, and put in prison. You risked ruining my life, Dave.

Dave I did it for you, Gemma.

Gemma Don't you dare! Don't you dare try and make me an excuse.

Dave I'm not. I wasn't.

Gemma Did you think I'd be impressed? Is that it? Coming home with all that money — did you think I'd be turned on or something?

Dave No.

Gemma That's it, isn't it? It always is with you. You think the more money you've got to wave about, the more sexy you are.

Dave (*embarrassed*) Gemma.

Gemma It's an ego trip — this whole thing. The money, being in a gang, pointing a gun at people. Make you feel big, did it?

Dave No. It wasn't like that.

Gemma No? (*To John*) What about you? Make you feel big and powerful, did it? Having a gun in your hand? Is that why you hit him? 'Cos you felt big for once in your sad life?

Gillian That's not fair. (*She pulls up a chair and sits next to John*)

Gemma Isn't it?

Dave Nobody was supposed to get hurt.

Gemma But they did, though, didn't they?

Philip It was just a tap on the head, that's all. He wasn't seriously injured.

Gemma How do you know that? How do you know he hasn't had a heart attack? How do you know he hasn't gone into a coma?

Philip He was all right. Believe me.

John Are you sure, Philip? Are you sure he was all right?

Philip Absolutely. Don't worry about him. He's going to be a hero. He'll probably get an award for bravery. He'll be living off this for years. They all will. It's probably the most exciting thing that's ever happened to any of them.

Dave Yeah, Phil's right. Come on, Gem, I'll admit we've been a bit reckless ...

Gemma Huh!

Dave And maybe it was stupid. But, well, we've got all this money sitting here ... (*He reaches for the bag*)

Gemma Don't touch it! Don't even think about it.

Dave What?

Gemma You're not having a penny of it.

Dave What d'you mean?

Gemma It's going back, all of it.

Dave But, we can't do that.

Gemma Why not? You were bold enough to go in and take it. Giving it back should be a breeze.

Philip Yes, and I'm sure the police would be completely understanding. "Sorry, Officer, we were a bit naughty, but we've realized the error of our ways." "That's all right, lads, just don't do it again, eh?"

Gemma Don't get sarcastic with me, I don't like it.

Philip Sorry. But exactly how are we supposed to return a bagful of stolen money without getting caught?

Gemma I don't know. You're obviously the mastermind of this little gang — you work it out.

Philip I don't think so. We've worked hard, taken a lot of risks, to get this money. We're not about to just hand it back, even if there was a way. Come on, Gemma, I know you're still feeling somewhat shocked about this whole thing, but the deed's been done, the die is cast.

Gemma What's that supposed to mean?

Philip It means that whatever happens, Dave here is already a criminal. We all are. We have committed a serious crime, and nothing is going to change that. You may not like it — and I can understand that — but come on, Gemma, why not take advantage of the situation?

Dave Yeah. Think about it, Gem: I could get you that BMW you've always wanted. Get a conservatory built. Holiday out in the Bahamas. New clothes ...

Gemma You idiot, Dave. You don't get it, do you? That stuff doesn't matter to me. You've always thought that it does, but it doesn't. Buying me things doesn't impress me. God, I only have to snap my fingers and out comes your credit card. It's so easy it's pathetic. All you've ever done is try and buy my affection. Well, I'm sorry, but it doesn't work. If you really want to win me over, if you really want to impress me, you'll pick up that bag and go and hand it in somewhere. You needn't get caught. Come on, Dave, show me you've got some backbone. Show me I didn't marry a complete tosser.

A moment as Dave deliberates. He looks from Gemma to John to Philip, and back to Gemma. He starts to get up, but Philip places his hands on his shoulders and sits him firmly back down

Philip Just a minute, Dave — before you go making any rash decisions. If you want to return your share of the money to the police, then OK, that's up to you. But this is a three-way split. You're not taking my share.
Dave I didn't say I was.
Philip What about you, John? You going to let Dave take away your chance of happiness? After all you've been through to get it?
Dave Hold on, hold on. I never said I was going to, did I?
Gemma You prat, Dave.
Dave No. I mean, I can't ... I don't ... The thing is ...
John You can take mine back. I don't want it.
Dave Eh?
Philip John?
John I don't want the money. I don't want any part of it. I just want to go back to being who I was before. Sorry.
Philip But you can't do that, John. You can't turn the clock back.
John I knew it was wrong. I said that right from the start. Not that I blame you, Philip, for talking me into it. I knew what I was doing. I take full responsibility for my actions.
Gemma Some sense at last.
John I knew it was wrong, but I still went ahead and did it. What does that make me, eh? What kind of man does that make me?
Gillian John ...
John I'm no better than some mindless thug. Worse.
Gillian John, don't ——
John No, I feel ashamed of what I did. Ashamed. And if I should profit from what happened that would make me a hypocrite. I may have escaped the punishment of the law, but that doesn't mean ——
Gillian For God's sake John, stop being so bloody pompous!
John (*shocked*) Pardon?

Gillian (*getting up*) All this self-righteous torment you put yourself through. It was the same when you lost your job. "Why, oh why did I do it? Why did I falsify my expenses?" Every day and night spent grappling with your conscience. Constantly apologizing to me — to the point where it became quite meaningless.

John Sorry.

Gillian You did something wrong, John, you got caught, you paid the price. End of story. (*A little pause*) Well, at least this time you seem to have got away with it. Let's make the most of that. Let's keep the money.

John Well ... I don't know. I mean, if you think ——

Gillian Yes, I do. Very much. Let's keep the money, John. Let's go away somewhere and be thoroughly reckless with it.

Gemma Have you gone soft, Gillian?

Gillian No. I don't think so. As Philip said, we can't turn the clock back. What's done is done. I see no advantage to anyone — other than the insurance companies — in returning the money. We may as well keep it and enjoy it.

Dave Yeah. She's got a point there, Gem.

Gemma Shut up, Dave. Listen, we don't know if they have got away with it yet. They might have been filmed. They could be on *Crimewatch* next week. At least if they give the money back the police wouldn't be so desperate to find them. In fact they probably wouldn't even bother.

Dave Yeah. That's true.

Gemma Besides, if you and Buster Edwards here go out recklessly spending money left, right and centre, I should think somebody might get a bit suspicious. You could both end up inside.

Gillian I'm prepared to take that chance. If you are, John.

John If that's what you want, Gilly. If that's what you really want. Of course, I will.

John and Gillian clasp hands

Gemma I think I'm gonna puke. Am I the only sane person in this room?

In the distance, the sound of a police siren can be heard, building

Listen, you two might be prepared to take that chance, but I'm not. This money — all of it — is going back. And if you haven't got the guts to do it, Dave, then ...

The siren now sounds like it's right outside, and a blue light flashes through the venetian blinds

Dave Oh, shit, it's the cops!

Philip Down! (*He grabs the gun off the table and peeks out of the window through the blinds*)

Dave, Gemma, John and Gillian all crouch down around the table. After a tense few moments the light disappears and the siren fades

Philip It's all right. They've gone.

Dave, still crouching low, joins Philip at the window and peeks out

Dave Are you sure, Phil? I mean, they could still be there — waiting for us to come out. Police marksmen on the rooftops, in bullet-proof vests. Oh shit. Is there a back way out of there?

Philip No, Dave, there isn't. Just shut up a minute. Let me think. (*He thinks*) Look, if they were after us, they would have kicked the door in by now, or at least told us to come out with our hands up, right? (*He looks out of the window*) Nothing. No cars, no marksmen on the rooftops. All quiet.

Dave Too quiet.

Gemma, John and Gillian all straighten up now

John What were you going to do, Philip, if they'd burst in on us?

Philip (*looking at the gun in his hand*) I don't know. I honestly don't know. Shout "bang" I suppose.

Gillian But if the police had burst in, and seen you holding that, I mean, if they'd been armed and ... Well ...

The implications of this have a sobering effect on Philip, and everyone else in the room. Philip lays the gun down — heavily — on the table. A moment

Gemma So, are you still hell-bent on keeping the money? Well? Do you really think it's worth going through this every time you hear a siren? Every time you see a policeman in the street? Every time there's a knock at the door? 'Cos that's how it's gonna be. You might well think you can just sit back and enjoy the money, but you never will. You'll be on the edge the whole time — waiting. Waiting for the moment when it all catches up with you. Think you can live with that? Right.

Gemma grabs the holdall off the table and heads for the door

Dave Gemma, wait. What are you gonna do?

Gemma Find somewhere to leave this bag, then ring the police and tell them where they can pick it up. After that I'm going home, packing a suitcase and going away.

Dave Away? Where away?

Gemma Don't know. My mother's maybe. Until I decide what to do with my future.

Dave Gem. Gemma. Please.

Gemma Don't try to phone me — as from now, we're not speaking. You staying here, Gillian, or do you want to come with me?

Gillian Staying.

Gemma Suit yourself. Personally I think you're mad, but ...

Gillian Take care, Gemma.

Gemma Yeah, you too. See yer. (*She opens the door*)

Philip Hold on, Gemma.

Gemma (*stopping and turning*) What?

Philip I'm sorry, but I can't let you go.

Gemma Beg your pardon?

Philip That's my money. I've gone through a lot to get it, and I am not going to let anybody take it away from me.

Gemma No? You gonna stop me?

Philip Don't make me.

Gemma What you gonna do? Shoot me in the back with your toy gun?

Philip (*with menace*) Give me the bag, Gemma. Now, please.

Everyone freezes. A momentary standoff. Then Philip suddenly lurches towards Gemma. Dave and John restrain him

Gemma exits

Dave No, Phil!

John Leave it, Philip! Let it go. It's all over.

Dave and John manage to push Philip back, down on to the bed

Dave Gemma!

Dave rushes out after Gemma

(*Off*) Gemma!

Dave returns a few moments later. She's gone. He walks slowly to the table and sits down

There is a long, heavy silence in the room

Gillian (*eventually*) Would anyone like a cup of tea?
John Tea? No, thanks. Is there any of that Scotch left?
Gillian Scotch? Er, yes. (*She hands John the bottle and the cups*) Are you
   planning on getting drunk?
John Drunk? No. We just need to ... You know.
Gillian Right. (*She moves to the window*) It's stopped raining now.
John Has it?
Gillian Why don't I go and see if I can get a taxi?
John Yes. That's probably a good idea. I won't be long.

John helps Gillian with her coat. She heads for the door

Gillian (*stopping by the door*) Gemma was probably right, you know. About
   keeping the money. It's not just a matter of getting away with it, is it?
   You've got to be able to live with your — your indiscretions. Otherwise
   ... Well. Anyway. I'll be outside, John.

Gillian exits

*John sits at the table and pours out three shots of Scotch. Both Philip and
Dave look totally crushed*

Dave (*his head down*) Shit.
John Sorry?
Dave I said "shit". As in shit.
John Oh.
Dave It's all gone pear-shaped. Everything pear-shaped.
John Pear-shaped? Yes, I suppose it has.
Dave (*close to tears*) If she leaves me — for good — I don't know what I'll
   do.
John It'll be all right. She's just a bit overwrought at the moment.
Dave All I ever wanted to do was make things easy for her. Give her a decent
   lifestyle. You know what I mean?
John Yes, Dave. I know what you mean. (*He hands Dave a Scotch*)

Dave downs the Scotch in one gulp

Dave Your missus seems to have taken it all very well.
John Gilly? Yes, she has. She ... She never ceases to amaze me.
Dave You're a lucky man, John. A very lucky man.
John Lucky? Well, I don't know about that, but ... Look, I was thinking
   about making a phone call — to Jarvis and Klein. Just to see if that chap
   was, you know ... Make sure he's all right.

Dave Is that a good idea?
John No? No. There might be something on the radio? I mean, if anything serious happened, they'd say, wouldn't they?
Dave Maybe. Best not to dwell on it.
John (*dwelling on it*) No, I suppose not.

Philip gets up, goes to the table and sits with Dave and John

Philip I'm sorry.
John Philip?
Philip I really am sorry.
Dave Sorry? We're all sorry, Phil. Look at us.
Philip I meant …
Dave Look, we knew what we were getting ourselves into.
John That's right. No-one blames you for anything.
Dave After all, it was our wives who threw the spanner in the works, wasn't it? Turning up like that.
John I couldn't believe it when I walked through the door and saw Gilly standing there.
Dave I nearly shat meself when I saw Gemma.
John We never did find out how they came to be here, did we?
Dave No. No, we didn't. One of us must have slipped up somewhere.
Philip The only person who's slipped up is me. This was my idea, my plan. I thought I'd covered every eventuality. Obviously not. I'm sorry.
Dave Will you stop apologizing? You're beginning to sound like John.
Philip Everything I've put you through, everything that's happened, and there's nothing to show for it. Nothing.

They ponder on this for a moment

Dave We did it, though, didn't we? Eh?
John Yes. Yes, we did.
Dave I mean, we may not have anything to show for it, but at least we can say we actually did it. How many people can say that, eh?
John Not very many, I shouldn't imagine.
Philip Trouble is, neither can we.
Dave What?
Philip We can't ever tell anyone what we've done, can we?
Dave No, I suppose not. Shame. I'd love to see people's faces.
John Quite a conversation piece, really.
Dave Yeah. Blinder.
Philip You won't though, will you?
Dave What? Oh, no. Course not. What d'you think I am, stupid? No, I won't say a word. But I won't forget it though. I'll remember this day for the rest of my life.

Philip I think we all will. One way or another.

John (*getting up*) Well, I suppose I'd better be ... Gilly's probably waiting in a taxi for me.

Dave Going straight home?

John Yes. You?

Dave Well, to be honest I feel like going out and getting completely bladdered. But, I suppose I ought to get back home. I might catch Gemma, before she ... Could you drop us at the station?

John Can do.

Dave Cheers. Nice one. (*He gets up*)

John Philip?

Philip Eh?

John What are you going to do now?

Philip Me? Well, I'm all out of hare-brained schemes for the time being. *So*, back to grinding reality, I suppose: the debts, the dull routine, the mediocrity ...

John No, I meant right now. Did you want to come with us?

Philip Thanks, but no. I'll stay here for a while. Clear up.

John Right.

Dave Sure?

Philip Yeah.

Dave Right.

John Thanks, Philip.

Philip Thanks? For what?

John I don't know, really. I just meant ... Well ...

Dave He means thanks for ... You know. For — just, thanks. OK?

Philip OK. (*He gets up*)

They all shake hands

Dave Give me a call, yeah?

Philip Sure.

John Perhaps we could all meet up over the Christmas holiday?

Philip Perhaps.

Dave Yeah.

Dave and John exit

Philip is left, deep in thought, for a moment. Then he downs his Scotch, and takes the bottle and cups back to the cabinet. There is the sound of footsteps coming down the steps outside, and a key in the lock. Philip turns

The door opens and Gemma walks in, carrying the holdall

They look at each other — their faces betraying absolutely nothing. She places the holdall on the table. Philip crosses to her. They kiss, passionately

Gemma It worked.
Philip Yeah.
Gemma It bloody worked!
Philip Just about.
Gemma You OK?
Philip Yeah. You?
Gemma Drained. But, I dunno, on a high. Look at me — I'm shaking. I feel like screaming my head off! I feel like ... I tell you what I feel like. (*She throws her jacket on to the bed then starts to unbutton Philip's shirt*)
Philip No. (*He sits down at the table*)
Gemma What's wrong?
Philip Nothing. I'm just a bit tense, that's all.
Gemma Yeah, I know. I've had a knot the size of a fist in here all day. (*She moves round and massages his neck*) You were good today. You were really good.
Philip So were you. Very convincing.
Gemma Felt like I was fighting a losing battle at times. When Gillian turned round and said she wanted to keep the money — God, that really floored me. I wasn't expecting that at all. She's full of surprises, that one.
Philip Yeah. Arrgh!
Gemma Sorry. God, you are tense aren't you?
Philip Very.
Gemma Well, it's all over now. We can relax.
Philip Can we?
Gemma What's up?
Philip Nothing. (*He gets up and picks up the bag*) Have you counted it?
Gemma Only quickly. I reckon about one-fifty, give or take.
Philip Not as much as we hoped.
Gemma Enough, though. Just be thankful we don't have to split it three ways.
Philip I guess.
Gemma For God's sake, Philip, what is wrong with you? Your plan worked. We've got the money.
Philip I know.
Gemma So?
Philip I just feel a little bit ...
Gemma What?
Philip Doesn't matter.
Gemma Guilty? Please don't tell me you feel guilty.
Philip I feel guilty.

Gemma Great.

Philip Sorry.

Gemma Well, I bloody don't. Dave deserves everything he gets. He was cheating on me long before we got together — and boasting about it. It was you who told me, remember?

Philip Yeah.

Gemma And as for John — what was it you called him? Dead from the neck down. The man has no life in him. He wouldn't know what to do with the money.

Philip It's not just about the money, Gemma.

Gemma No, it's not. It's about us. Me and you, and our chance of escape. Look, by the time their tiny little minds have worked out what's happened we'll be long gone. Out of this cold, grey little country, away from all the cold, grey little people. Your words, Philip, those are your words.

Philip I know. I know what I said.

Gemma Don't wimp out on me now.

Philip I'm not wimping out.

Gemma What then?

Dave's mobile phone rings offstage; the unmistakable trill

Philip What's that?

Gemma Sounds like … Oh, shit!

Gemma rushes out to the kitchen and returns with Dave's mobile

Philip Their stuff. They didn't take their stuff!

Gemma Shit! Philip, what are we … ?

Philip Shut up! Let me think.

The phone stops ringing

Did you see them go?

Gemma Yes. Together. In a taxi. I waited.

Philip OK, so they've realized they left their stuff behind, they turn round — they'll be on their way back …

Gemma We've got to get out of here! (*She grabs her coat and the bag and makes for the door*)

Philip Gemma, wait! I just need to think …

Gemma (*at the door*) Philip, there's no time. Come on!

Philip Gemma, no … !

Gemma swings open the door, and instantly steps backwards

John and Dave are framed in the doorway

Philip Dave. John. Come in.

Dave and John step inside

The Lights fade to Black-out

FURNITURE AND PROPERTY LIST

ACT I
Scene 1

On stage: Single fold-up bed with bare mattress
Kitchen table
Three unmatching chairs
Chest of drawers or cabinet. *On it*: bottle of Scotch, stack of plastic
cups. *In it*: two handguns
Old radiator

Off stage: Mug of tea (**Philip**)
Briefcase, carrier bag containing cans of beer (**Dave**)

Personal: **Philip**: wrist-watch, plastic laminated ID card
John: wrist-watch
Dave: wallet containing photograph, credit cards etc.; wrist-watch

Scene 2

Off stage: Cordless phone (**Gillian**)
Cordless phone (**Gemma**)

Scene 3

Re-set: Table and chairs against US wall

Set: New bottle of Scotch

Strike: Old bottle of Scotch, beer cans, mugs, **Dave**'s briefcase

Off stage: Large carrier bags with "J & K" logo containing raincoats, gloves and
woollen ski masks. *In one bag*: large canvas holdall (**Dave** and
John)

Personal: **Dave**: handgun, mobile phone
John: handgun, wallet containing photograph, credit cards etc.
Philip: key on piece of string

ACT II
Scene 1

Off stage: Two mugs of coffee (**Gillian**)

Scene 2

Re-set: Holdall and gun in centre of table

Off stage: Mug of tea (**Gillian**)

LIGHTING PLOT

Practical fitting required: naked light bulb pendant
One interior with exterior backing to window and front door, and interior backing to
door to kitchen and bathroom. Plus two areas either side of the set for **Gemma** and
Gillian in ACT I, Scene 2

ACT I, SCENE 1

To open: General interior lighting with bulb lit. Street lamp effect on exterior backing

Cue 1	**Philip**: "Are you in?" *Black-out*	(Page 19)

ACT I, SCENE 2

To open: Darkness

Cue 2	Telephone rings *Bring up spots on* **Gillian** *and* **Gemma** *on either side of the set*	(Page 20)
Cue 3	**Gemma**: "… I think we need to talk, don't you?" *Black-out*	(Page 21)

ACT I, SCENE 3

To open: General interior and exterior lighting

Cue 4	**Gemma**: "We wait, Gillian. We wait." Music *Slow fade to black-out*	(Page 29)

ACT II, SCENE 1

To open: General interior and exterior lighting. Fade exterior lights during scene to
suggest rain

Cue 5	**Gillian**: "John!" *Black-out*	(Page 40)

ACT II, SCENE 2

To open: General interior lighting with practical bulb lit. Exterior lighting darker

Cue 6	Siren sounds as if it's right outside *Blue light flashes through blinds*	(Page 45)
Cue 7	They crouch around the table. Pause *Blue light fades*	(Page 46)
Cue 8	**Dave** and **John** step inside *Fade to black-out*	(Page 53)

EFFECTS PLOT

ACT I

Cue 1   **John**: "Mmm."   (Page 13)
Toilet flushes

Cue 2   As ACT I SCENE 2 begins   (Page 20)
Telephone rings

Cue 3   **Philip**: "OK, so where were we …?"   (Page 24)
Mobile phone with novelty ringtone rings

Cue 4   **Gemma**: "We wait, Gillian. We wait."   (Page 29)
Music

ACT II

Cue 5   **Gemma** moves to the cabinet   (Page 31)
Sound of rain fades up very slowly as scene progresses

Cue 6   **Philip** puts the bottle and cups back on the cabinet   (Page 38)
Toilet flushes

Cue 7   Black-out   (Page 40)
Sound of rain fades

Cue 8   As ACT II SCENE 2 begins   (Page 40)
Restore sound of rain; fade as scene progresses

Cue 9   **Gemma**: "Am I the only sane person in this room?"   (Page 45)
Police siren, building

Cue 10   **Gemma**: " … the guts to do it, Dave, then …"   (Page 46)
Police siren reaches maximum

Cue 11   They crouch around the table. Pause   (Page 46)
Siren fades

Cue 12   **Gemma**: "What then?"   (Page 52)
Mobile phone with novelty ringtone rings

Cue 13   **Philip**: "Shut up! Let me think."   (Page 52)
Phone stops ringing

Milton Keynes UK
Ingram Content Group UK Ltd.
UKHW021827090823
426601UK00010B/637